40 DAYS AND 40 NIGHTS:

FROM BROKENNESS TO RESTORATION

A Poetry Collection

Kayvonna K. Stigall

40 Days and 40 Nights: From Brokenness to Restoration
Copyright © 2018 Kayvonna K. Stigall

All rights reserved. No part of this book may be copied or reproduced in any form without written permission from the publisher.

Cover design: Keith Martin
www.martin-multimedia.com
: Creativelogo art
Bio Pic: Janell Green, Da'Vis Images

ISBN: 978-1-937400-64-4

Printed in the United States of America

Published by Manifold Grace Publishing House, LLC
Southfield, Michigan 48033
www.manifoldgracepublishing.com

Acknowledgments

I'm grateful to the one and only true and living God, Jesus Christ, for allowing me to use my gift to be a witness and spread His Word to the world.

I would like to thank my husband, my rock, my partner and friend, Karl. During this season of growth in our marriage, which I did not see coming, God truly showed me who I was. He showed me that I needed to trust that He has equipped you to love and care for me in ways I thought you could not. It has been a year of humbling, grace, mercy, trials, tests and restoration. I love you. To God be the glory!

Table of Contents

Acknowledgments	v
40 Days and 40 Nights: Can I Testify?	1
The Broken Years	3
The Creaking of the Door	5
Drowning of the Night	6
I'm All the Way Up	7
Don't Faint Now	8
But I'm Just Tripping	9
It's Not Your Story	10
I was Made Just Right	12
He Made No Mistakes – So Stay Out My Make-up	13
Survey Says	14
I'm Gucci	15
Dream On	16
The Original "Clap Back"	17
Allow Me to Introduce Myself	18
Garbage Day	20
Hold On	22
The Tainted Beauty Mark	24
Jesus	25
I'm Hurt, But I Gotta Work	26
There's a Fire, But I Don't Smell Smoke	27
I'm Still Standing	29
There is Healing – in the Ugly Cry	30
Loose Ends	31
It's Going to Cost You Something	32
Everyday Kind of Love	34
An Open Heart to Love	35
In a Love So Strong	36
Wife to Husband (To My Husband Karl)	37
Wedding Day	38
Jesus is Love	39

Double Life	40
Spirit Break Out	42
Life's Journey	43
When I'm Alone	44
When I Write	45
About the Author	47

40 Days and 40 Nights

Can I Testify?

The title of this book, *40 Days and 40 Nights*, came straight from heaven to my ears. I was lying in bed with my brand new blank journal. I had just finished praying and was getting ready to do some writing. Reflecting on my day, I heard, "40 Days and 40 Nights." I opened the composition notebook and wrote down the different titles for some of the poetry pieces in this book, which God spoke to me. I was then led to research some of the symbolism of the number 40 in the Bible.

The number 40 is mentioned in the Bible 146 times. It generally symbolizes a period of testing, trial or probation.

During Moses' life, he lived forty years in Egypt and forty years in the desert before God delivered his people out of slavery.

Moses was also on Mount Sinai for forty days and forty nights on two separate occasions (Exodus 24:18, 34:1-28) receiving God's laws. He also sent spies, for forty days, to investigate the land God promised the Israelites as an inheritance (Numbers 13:25, 14:34).

Jonah warned Nineveh for forty days that its destruction would come because of the many sins of the land.

The prophet Ezekiel laid on his right side for forty days to symbolize Judah's sins (Ezekiel 4:6).

Jesus was tempted by the devil, not just three times, but many times during the forty days and forty nights he fasted just before his ministry began.

Jesus appeared to His disciples and others for forty days after His resurrection from the dead.[1]

After researching, I reflected on my year. It was filled with so many changes, and ups and downs. I then realized that it had been full of trials, tests, obstacles, anxiety, fear and doubt. Most of the titles here represent a lot of what my year has taught me about myself, who I am and what God has called me to do. In this season, it's my time to trade up, turning in brokenness for restoration. These poems are a part of my journey.

---

[1] www.biblestudy.org – Meaning of Numbers in the Bible – the Number 40

The Broken Years

You were supposed to dry tears from the start,
But you allowed malice into your heart.
Nights that should have been family times and family ties
Turned into cold, v-shaped lurking eyes.
Solitude crying smiles,
Whispered prayers, which seemed to fall on night's darkness,
And the trees' dead foundation left over from the winter's brutal victory over the fall.
The broken years.

The years of hard goodbyes
And weeping, and roller coaster shoulders
That couldn't hold up mountains.
Thoughts of the broken crumbs of stale manna,
Which slipped through crooked lined fingers
Of discouragement, disgust and disturbed peace.
Oh, but the broken years!

The broken years birthed a seed—
A seed that was watered by tears and nurtured by trembling hands.
A seed whose glow was created by the light of hope and prayers;

Not the world's hope.
"Hope I make it!"
"Hope they don't forget me!"
No, the hope that comes from the flipped coin side of faith,
And the mercies of a God, who has endless time and unwavering grace.
It withstands the inconsistency of man's shadowed imitation of agape love and true mournful embraces of change.
He, and He alone, restoreth the broken years.

The Creaking of the Door

Slightly open in the midst of it all,
Time in between the sounds.
Subtle, yet repetitive reminders of the storms of the past.
Constant nagging of the losses and down times.
Will the hallways of comfort not bow to the creaking of the door?
Surely, the quick footsteps pounding up the stairs can give way to
Enough vibration to silence the creaking of the door.
Or the words being released, like nails followed by hammers, to secure the hurt and leave a
Foundation of pain and insecurities, supported by beams of generational curses and,
"You acting just like yo…" accusation verses.
Keeping silences on the stove, like a boiling pot of rice as the foam rises up,
But it's only an implosion 'cause there is no substance to your actions, your words or your blame.
So, the creak in the door remains the same.

Drowning of the Night

Night sky covers a bleeding heart and sleepless soul.
It can lose control and be as free as a bird's gliding wing,
Or as still as a star positioned to shine on its own stage.
But, the drowning of the night is two-fold.
Have you ever tried to drown out the night?
Where the tears of the heart and the pulse of the soul
Meet to entangle in what should sing praises to thee,
only true and living God,
But finds itself drowning in the sounds of gun shots,
hate, smog and
The day-to-day uncertainty of a nation whose money
yields to, "In God We Trust."
But it won't kneel to, "We Trust in God."
So we drown out the night.
What night are you drowning out?
And how do you feel when you wake up?

I'm All the Way Up!

Looking to the sky, from whence cometh my help, for sure.
Embracing yet another scar I've had to endure.
Will it heal? Yes! Did it hurt? Yes!
But that does not diminish its value any less.

I'm all the way up! Up in my joy!
Up in faith and hope!

Turn down for what?
Let God's fiery boldness consume you.
Stand still in Him, but continue to move
As He leads you.

All the way up,
So stay lit with His love.
It's more than just a fad;
It's everlasting from above.

Don't Faint Now

Worn out minds.
Thoughts of defeat swaddling every inkling of
motivation to keep moving.
Daylight only bringing forth a new set of problematic
equations and fractions—
And you have not even seen an equal sign
Or a pencil-drawn multiplication of anything positive.
Drought—drier than a desert, or the rusted ridges of
your esophagus while
Trying to take a drink of powdered milk
On a hot day, in a snowsuit,
In the corner of an inferno.
I know. All bad.
Yet, you still have days—days that are numbered, yet
possibilities are endless.
Don't faint in your dry place.

But I'm Just Trippin'

So, they can be a bit much, but who isn't?
If you have been here on this earth for any given time, somebody has been irritated by you.
Okay, I won't leave it there. Let's do this instead:

Are you breathing?
Are you reading these words?
Then surely, you are a candidate for what you just heard.
#ijs #sorrynotsorry #turnthepage

It's Not Your Story

I won't let anyone rewrite my story.
No one was there for every part;

They cannot truly read your heart.
Though some pieces may be visible for the eyes to see,
Some are so shattered they're only for God and me.

See, I get up every day and hand those pieces to Him.
He never turns them away or makes light of them.
He carefully guides me, without exposing a trace
Of the pain given or received—they are protected by
His mercy and grace.

When the sun goes down, knees, too.
God lays those pieces out in my devotion so that they can be ministered to.
See, those pieces are my testimony.
They keep me humble and at peace.
I don't look at them as my weaknesses.
They are extensions of me.

Misplaced brokenness can keep you in a place of pity and bitterness.
It can cause you to live in cycles of constant self-

righteousness.
Let God's love be your place where your tears flow like rain.
Allow Him to carry all of the pain.
It will free you to live, not just be alive;
To be a witness to someone else
And overcome,
Not just survive.

I Was Made Just Right

God doesn't make mistakes.
I was fearfully and wonderfully made.
From the top of my head to the soles of my feet,
When God created me, I was complete.

I am proud to be the "she," the "her" He made me to be.
To believe He is all-knowing, I have to confess I am "she."

He Made No Mistakes!

So, Stay Out My Make-Up!

Since I'm already convinced that God makes no mistakes,
It's just a waste of your time trying to change what just ain't.
No, I won't be lukewarm and agree to be friendly,
Because the Holy Spirit lives within me.

I'm not afraid of losing friends,
Nor being blocked.
My conviction runs deeper than
Facebook live, shares, likes and Photoshop.

#Hemakesnomistakes #Iamshe

Survey Says

Survey Says:

Jesus is Lord!
Jesus made you great!
You were not built to break.
You are an overcomer.
You are more than a conquer in Christ Jesus.
The devil is a liar!
The devil is the father of lies!
Jesus will keep you in perfect peace, if you keep your mind stayed on Him.
Jesus is the one true and living God.
Jesus is your help.
Jesus is a mother to the motherless.

I approve this message!

"I'm Gucci! I'm Good, Doing Fine, Cool!"

So, in all things, get an understanding. Words are my friends.
I wanted to know what this meant, "I'm Gucci, man!"

This young guy crossed my path as I was also in motion,
Trying to dig in my purse for my coconut lotion.

In the process of us both moving, I brushed against his hand.
Me: "Sorry, excuse me."
Him: "Oh, I'm Gucci, man!"

No longer is Gucci just an Italian luxury brand.
It is now an adjective: "I'm Gucci, man!"

Dream On

Through rejection, insecurities and what your eyes can see,
Dream on!

Past hurt, pain and tears,
Dream on!

Pushing down fears, doubt and self—yes, *you*,
Dream on!

While you're dreaming, don't forget to live on.
That's the only way your dreams will come true!

The Original "Clap Back"

The Original "Clap Back" was between Jesus and the enemy.
Yes, the devil, our only adversary.
See, he tried to tempt Jesus, tried to get into His head.
But what he got was some clap backs instead.
See, he thought he could fool Jesus to thinking He needed him,
Just like the world tries to get us to believe that, without its vices,
Our life would be dim.
If we all would truly believe that this world's provisions are just tools,
That there is only one source, Jesus Christ, we wouldn't keep falling for the enemy's
Clap backs, which continue to make us look like fools.
He uses them to make us believe that he has some control,
Like a person who tries to get you to buy something that's already been sold;
Like a person trying to give you your shoes, when they're already on your feet;
Or trying to give you cake, when you're on your second piece.
He can't give you what God already says is yours.
He has no power. Who needs keys to open doors?
Without God's permission, the devil can't even be who he is.
He even believes in God—the greatest clap back. There it is! Drops the mic…

Allow Me to Introduce Myself

I am a comforter.
God is the ultimate comforter.
From grief to sadness and hurt,
They all are brought to their knees
By God's unchanging hand and love.

Allow me to introduce myself:
I am love.
God has agape love for us.
His love is unconditional,
Judgment-free zone.

Allow me to introduce myself:
I am Joy.
You may not always be happy,
But because joy comes from the Lord,
It gives you strength and power
To not let your feelings consume you.

Allow me to introduce myself:
I am a provider—
Not just of material things,
But *all* things.

To keep you whole physically, financially, mentally and spiritually.
Allow me to introduce myself:
I am forgiveness.
God is a God of, not a second chance,
But another chance.
Take His forgiveness and walk in righteousness.

Allow me to introduce myself:
I am love, joy, a provider, a comforter, a healer, a forgiver and so much more.
Now that I've introduced myself, get to know me for yourself.
The one and only, true and living God, better known as Jesus—also known as The Holy Spirit.

Garbage Day

It's garbage day every day, somewhere in the world,
all the time.
I don't want your garbage to show up on mine.
See, we all have problems and concerns that can get
in the way.
But I am not the elected official for garbage day.

If I invite you into my space, that is voluntarily
submission.
I've just given you garbage-dumping permission.
So that my metaphors and rhyming verses won't get
in the way,
Let me give you some real talk about garbage day.

See, garbage is all the negative and whining about
what life has done.
Some people whine when it's cloudy, then whine if it's
too much sun.
They have a tantrum when they don't get their way,
then they go on Facebook and other
Media and commence to garbage day.
Leaving cups open with dirt about their ex and his
new boo flowing out.
If ya don't care so much, why is it all you talk about?

Crumbled wrappers with sticky gum exposing you can be crazy and cool.
Then, ten minutes later, a post makes you look like a fool
With a hashtag "#don'tjudgeme"
You could have written a book with your status updates. We have read your whole life story
because you laid it out, like ten full buffet plates.
Then, you get mad when someone hits the reply, like they pick-locked your diary and exposed a lie.
A diary, what a notion! It's become a lost art.
Now we trust Facebook with our vulnerable parts.

The enemy has the airways and is using them as his puppets and props.
We have replaced prayer and worship with selfie time, status updates and Photoshop.
Apps, quizzes and media testimonies.
Yes, it can be a great tool, but also very time-consuming.
Don't be distracted and miss the most important status update of all:
"Jesus is soon to return!" No reply needed at all.

Hold On

Can I Testify?

I wrote this song while I was sitting in my car. It was raining, and I had just finished putting my groceries in my car. I was thinking about how tired I was, and I just wanted to go home and go to sleep. Then, I thought even further into my tiredness. I not only wanted to go home and go to sleep for the night. I wanted to sleep for much longer—like a week. I could hear the Holy Spirit say, "Hold on." While sitting in my car, I wrote these lyrics.

(Verse)
I've tried to be more than me,
But I found out
That's not being free.
But if I let go,
And stand on His Word,
There is nothing I can't endure.
(Chorus)
If you just hold on,
It will be alright.

Just trust His plan.
Stay in the fight. It won't be long.
He is right there.
Don't you give up. Cast on Him your cares.
(Verse)
This world is not eternity.
It changes, and it won't always be.
So, if you feel defeated and your
Spirit is down, lift your head up
And rise above the clouds.
(Chorus)
'Cause if ya just hold on,
It will be alright.
Trust His plan. Stay in the fight.
It won't be long. He is right there.
Don't you give up. Cast on Him your cares.
(Special)
My tears have been translated.
Your blood, it covers me.
Your arms are open wide.
My brokenness received.
(Chorus)
If ya just hold on,
It will be alright.
Just trust His plan. Stay in the fight.
It won't be long. He is right there.
Don't you give up. Cast on Him your cares.
Hold on.

Tainted Beauty Mark

Because it was the beauty that set the stage for pain, discomfort and hurt.
It was the last thing that wanted to be up front and center.

Compliments no longer created warm smiles and soft nods. They became daggers of reflections of times not so pleasant.

Being looked over and passed by seemed to be the best intrinsic reward—and safe.

Safe from roaming eyes and lying tongues, safe from deceitful whispers of things not even known in this innocence.

The Lord has now restored the tainted beauty mark,

His blood bringing forth truth, light and forgiveness

Forgiveness beyond this world's understanding;

Only the forgiveness found under the covenant.

Lord: The Covenant Keeper!

Jesus

As my eyes swell with tears,
I try my best to embrace peace.
Even with a trembling ear and stuttering lip,
I keep on smiling to bring hope to all that's missin'.
I wish that I could tell my story through my sighs,
And that my words could be translated through my eyes.
But, since this world can only feel what it can see,
I have to reach beyond this atmosphere to grab what's real.

Jesus, I'm the apple of your eye.
Jesus, and you're the reason I can stand.
Jesus, there's no question in my mind.
Jesus, not just a man, but a Spirit, an unchanging hand.

As the day surrenders to the night,
My heart turns with bended knee.
Though my spirit may be weak,
In His arms is where I have perfect peace.

Jesus, I'm the apple of your eye.
Jesus, and you're the reason I can stand.
Jesus, there's no question in my mind.
Jesus, not just a man, but a Spirit, an unchanging hand.

I'm Hurt, But I Gotta Work

The thought of pain can cause a spirit to close up in the fetal position;
Yet, many work while in pain.
Pain from life, death and everything in between.
Choosing love over hate, forgiveness over revenge,
And hope over defeat.

I'm hurt, but I gotta work.

Shattered pieces can produce a great picture frame,
Guided by the hand of God to ensure the placement
Of every sliver of its healed pain.

Work through the pain. Love through the stains.
Care through the scars.
Let God's rain clean the elusive parts of your soul.
You have work to do.

There's a Fire! But, I Don't Smell Smoke!

Flames filled with heat, distressed;
Consumed in my own premeditated mess.
Dark shadows being relieved by the call of a fire.
So hot that it instigates to fight against its own fury, trying to escape.

Yet, I don't smell the smoke.
Surely, it would have choked me by now.
No doubt, I should be a memory, a story, an obituary.
Yet, I am still here—*standing*, at that.

Though the fire burns on, I don't inhale what this life has,
So, I don't smell smoke.
Refusing to conform,
So, I don't smell smoke.
Standing in faith,
So, I don't smell smoke.
Trusting God's Word, the *whole* Word,
So, I don't smell smoke.

What is the smoke?
It's distractions.
Stay focused on the clouds.
That's where the rain will come from.

The rain—

It represents life, growth, new things, a cleansing;
God's falling hope on His people,
Who see the rainbow in all of its beauty and know that it
Represents His promise, as He validated moons before
People started inhaling the smoke.

We cannot pretend that we don't see the
Fires in the world, but we don't have to inhale
The *smoke*.

I'm Still Standing

The days can take more than days.
Hope can take more than faith.

A life can change without permission.
So, it's best to know every season.
Situations bring possibilities.
And conversation births opportunities.
With all that we can see and know,
It's best to stand still.

Stand still in storms of crying pain.
Stand still in scars of falling rain.
Stand still in knee-bending faith.
Stand still, stand strong—hold on.

Healing in the Ugly Cry

Let the make-up run.
Let the tear ducts dry.
There is truly healing in the ugly cry.

Praise and worship,
Singing, dancing.
Raising hands up high.
There is healing in the ugly cry.

Not for show,
Not for fashion.
Just letting go of this world's
Critiquing eye.
Sometimes, it takes all that,
Then some.
So, let go. Do the ugly cry.

Loose Ends

Two strings, twisted and unraveling at a speed unknown.
Winding roads, connecting with no sign of direction
To prevent an accident.
Loose ends.

A pair of untamed bull dogs,
Released in a field of freshly grown daises.
Loose ends.

Loose ends produce messy results.
It's not so much *where* they are;
It's *what* they are.

Loose ends produce messy thoughts.
It's not so much *how* they are.
It's *when* they are. Beware of loose ends.
They are bound to show up anywhere.
No pun intended.

It's Going to Cost You Something

Nothing costs more than love!
The heart rings loud and true.
Eager uncertain lips to kiss.
The passing of lies to trust.
How can the arms *catch*?
Yet, still, it allows love through.

Everything and everyone has to "go through."
But, nothing keeps us more unified than love.
How can life's circumstances *catch*?
Society's lack of control is true.
The passing of lies to trust.
Deceit is sealed with a kiss.

Who gives this venom kiss
That we let pass through,
Compromising our trust,
Disguised as help and love?
Who validated it as truth?
Who approved the *catch*?

Why do we always *catch*?
Catch hell, *catch* a cold, *catch* a kiss?
What much nowadays do we *catch* that is true?

Does acknowledging it make it *"all well"* regarding what we go through?
'Cause without it, there is no love.
And without love, there is no trust.

And without trust,
The springboard of hope will *not catch,*
Nor allow a running over or drizzle of love.
This, then, would produce a honey-glazed kiss,
Which would allow support and true hope to come through,
Validating that the love is free to flow true!

The people really only want what's true
Because then, they *can* trust.
That's the only thing that will bring them through.
They can be secure in the *catch,*
And enjoy the hydrated long-awaited kiss
That's represented by priceless love.

Invaluable love, all-encompassing and true.
Eloquent kiss fortified by trust,
And the *catch* letting all things hopeful
Run freely through.

Everyday Kind of Love

You hear people say, "Home is where the heart is."
Well, if this is true,

If the heart represents love, God is in your home, too.

For God is love, agape love, as a matter of fact.

Meaning, He loves you in all that you are, with no strings attached.

An Open Heart to Love

Agape love surrounds a world that, at times, has no embrace.
It contains God's unconditional yearning to be in first place.
His love reaches out to every woman, girl, boy and man.
And it's not confined or threatened by our circumstance.

It's a priceless gift, not bound by earthly chains.
Not tied up in feelings, nor placed in a box of "no change."
It's uncontainable by the world's laws and changing faces.
Reaches past sin's hell pit destination and different races.

Agape love is surely the love for one another—
Heart to heart, sisters and brothers.
As God had intended, He has the perfect plan;
Let us love unconditionally, reflect and offer to others
God's open arms and His open hands.

In a Love So Strong

Crooked gates with grains of grains.

Brokenness has its place in time.

Revealing all healing,

In a love so strong.

Cracked doors with squeaky knobs;

Insecurities have their place in time.

Revealing all strength,

In a love so strong.

Wife to Husband
(For Karl)

I am trapped in the whimsical thoughts of you.
Conquered by your kiss, captivated by the
Caress of the warmth of your soft hand.

Thinned clouds keep our day long together.
Oh, how the blue skies unendingness mimics my eternal
devotion to you!
Awkward smiles unknowing, but willing, with
Lingering touches fill the day.
A day well spent.
Setting the atmosphere.
For a forever love, man and woman, husband and wife,
Divinely placed and sealed by God's mercy and grace.

Love, Man and Woman, Man and Wife

My love for you reaches beyond this world's
understanding of love.
For we both are connected to an undying, never-failing
love, which can only be found, captivated
and blossomed in the bosom of Jesus Christ.
Flesh of my flesh,
Bone of my bone.
Forsaking all others with a genuine commitment to be
steadfast.
Forever yielded to loving you as Christ loves the church
shall be my daily devotion.
Flesh of my flesh,
Bone of my bone.
Love that is wrapped in humility and governed in Christ
can only
Flourish and grow, even in the midst of some blowing
winds and thunderous clouds.
Flesh of my flesh,
Bone of my bone.
Today is the beginning of a forever—*our* forever.
Forever committed to the journey of *us*.

Jesus is Love

Day and night, I pray,
Drifting in His arms.
Day and night, I pray,
Drifting in His arms.

Love, you are love.
Love, Jesus is love yah.
Love, you are love.
Love, Jesus is love.

Dreams and hopes stay clear
When your love is near.
Fear and doubt dry up
In the presence of your love!

You are love.
Love, Jesus is love yah.
Love, you are love.
Love, Jesus is love.

Your love is unconditional.
Your love is unconditional.
Your love is unconditional.
Jesus is love!

Double Life

It's hard living a double life,
So, I'm gonna keep it 100 and live for Jesus Christ.
See, He is that deal,
Standing in as our lawyer,
Stamping "Approved" on our appeals.
See, my rap sheet was long,
Some things written in invisible ink,
So folks wouldn't do what they do, and throw me
Under the sink.
Drag out my dirt and spray paint on my testimony,
Just to stop what was purposed and set up for His glory.
See, I would have quit a long time ago.
But the Holy Spirit in me sprang forth and took over the show,
Telling me it's bigger than me and its purpose is beyond my understanding.
It has straightened out crooked ways and allowed smooth landing.

So, keep with the truth. It's only proper to confess
That Jesus Christ is the only true and living God. Put your double life to rest.

Spirit, Break Out

And Lord, we ask you to plow the fields,
Leaving bountiful room for your spirit to yield.
To break out and run reckless in these vessels, your creation.
Tear down walls of division so heaven can come down and Reign over the nation!
The veil has been torn!
The blood has been shed!
Our Father, whose name is great,
Rules our thoughts, motives and our steps ahead!
Let your spirit run free,
Like the lily in a fresh cool wind—
Mending broken hearts, breaking bondages of sin!
Restraint? Be gone!
Unrestricted praise, spring forth!
Total spirit mayhem, begin your course!
For we can only win if we give Him our all!
So, let go of who *you* are, and let His Spirit break your fall!
Break out!

Life's Journey

Memories live through your eyes.

Time will tell their worth.

Sunshine can bend,

But trees of hope stand strong.

Lend your ears to truth.

Close your heart to doubt.

Let your soul overflow with peace,

And your hands bring forth humbleness.

Stay focused on the green grass,

And stand firm on the cracked road.

When I'm Alone

(read to the instrumental of "I Need Love" by LL Cool J)

When I'm alone in my room, sometimes I get on my knees,

So I can speak to my Father and say, "Help me please."

'Cause this world got me twisted with its angles and shoves,

And every day that I breathe, I know I need your love.

So, here I am, giggling about the past

Because my future's looking bettah and my witness on blast.

Got me flowing in the spirit, with no strings attached.

No bells or whistles needed 'cause your spirit is the catch.

Spittin' ink, Christ-driven and my focus is souls.

Gotta fill the new wine skins; throw out the old.

Fresh wind blowing, so you better catch a whiff.

No limits on His flow and no respect of person on His drift.

That means it's for *everybody*; take the lid off and be free!

No chains, no barriers or boundaries!

When I Write

I write when I write.
The ink is like my morning coffee
that I sometimes warm up midday,
and for a late-night dribble from my fingers.

I write when I write.
Words from my eyes, ears and nose,
create the senses of my flow.

I write when I write.
By leaving out the "g"
at times has been known
to spark even the hooded-kind.

I write when I write.
The process *is* a process,
so it's *always* "about."
Open to whatever it brings,
bringing whatever is open.

Whispers from God's angels—charged to me

"…and you will hear words from heaven."

About the Author

Kayvonna K. Stigall is a native of River Rouge, Michigan. She is married and has two children. She is a teacher, poet, songwriter and author. Her first book, *The Rise Above the Clouds*, a collection of poetry, was published in April of 2016.

40 Days and 40 Nights: From Brokenness to Restoration is a collection of poetry that tells of trials, tribulations, tests, brokenness, love and restoration. Kayvonna is the CEO of The Rise Above the Clouds, which is named after her first publication. She writes poetry for special occasions, performs poetry/spoken word, and conducts poetry writing workshops.

For more information, contact her at info@riseabovetheclouds.com or www.riseabovetheclouds.com.

www.ingramcontent.com/pod-product-compliance
Lightning Source LLC
Chambersburg PA
CBHW071757080526
44588CB00013B/2280